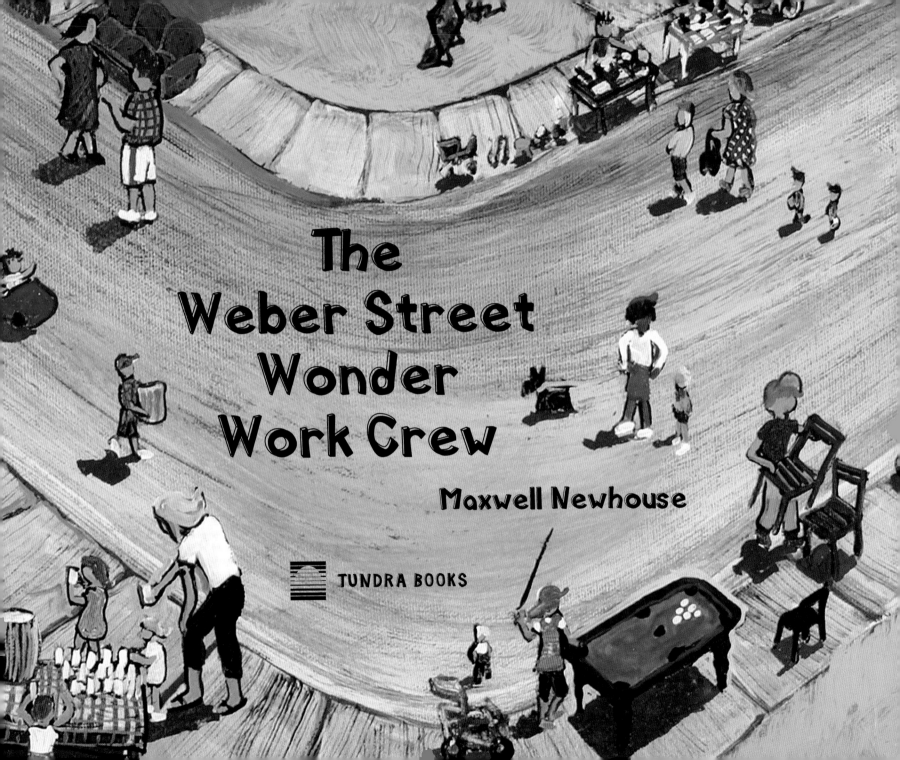

The
Weber Street
Wonder
Work Crew

Maxwell Newhouse

TUNDRA BOOKS

For my three grandsons: Coen, Cael, and Ryder Max

Published in Canada by Tundra Books,
75 Sherbourne Street, Toronto, Ontario M5A 2P9

Published in the United States by Tundra Books of Northern New York,
P.O. Box 1030, Plattsburgh, New York 12901

Library of Congress Control Number: 2009929060

Library and Archives Canada Cataloguing in Publication

Newhouse, Maxwell
The Weber Street wonder work crew / Maxwell Newhouse.
ISBN 978-0-88776-913-9
I. Title.
PS8627.E865W43 2010   jC813'.6   C2009-902976-6

We acknowledge the financial support of the Government of Canada through the Book Publishing Industry Development Program (BPIDP) and that of the Government of Ontario through the Ontario Media Development Corporation's Ontario Book Initiative. We further acknowledge the support of the Canada Council for the Arts and the Ontario Arts Council for our publishing program.

ONTARIO ARTS COUNCIL
CONSEIL DES ARTS DE L'ONTARIO

Medium: oil on canvas

Printed in China

1 2 3 4 5 6   15 14 13 12 11 10

We're the Weber Street Wonder Work Crew and we can make a difference!

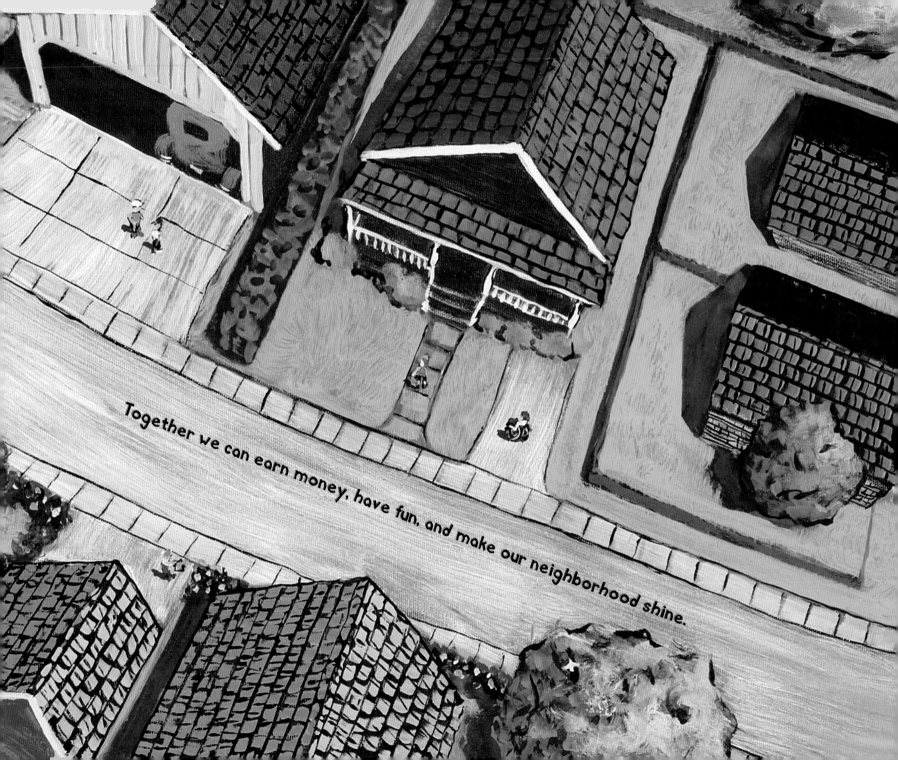

Together we can earn money, have fun, and make our neighborhood shine.

Sylvia's got a green thumb. She helps Mr. Flannigan in his garden.

His roses make Weber Street beautiful.

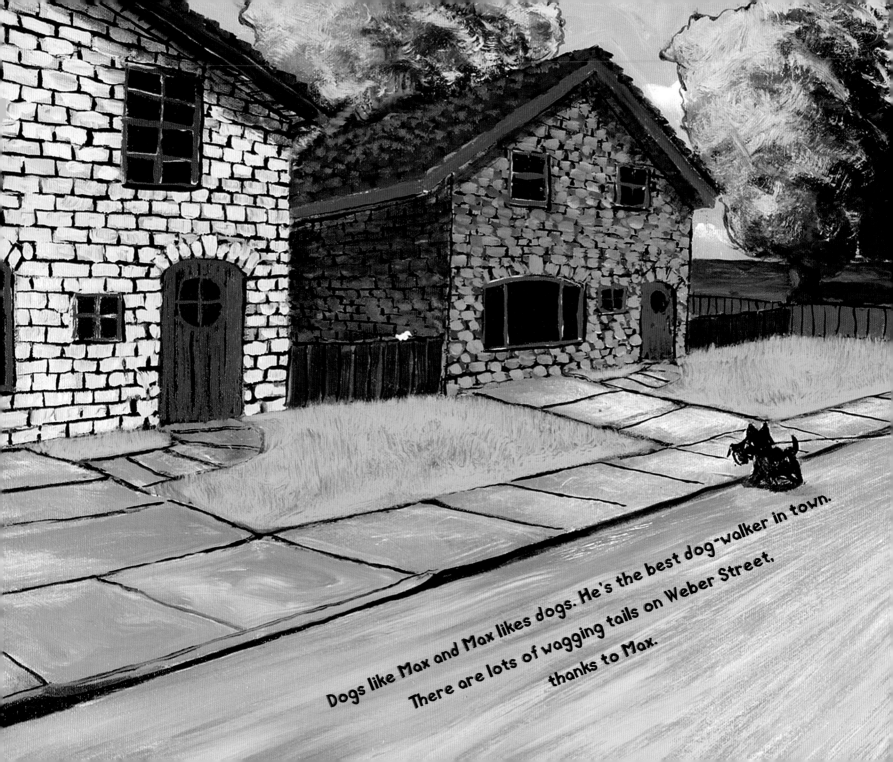

Dogs like Max and Max likes dogs. He's the best dog-walker in town. There are lots of wagging tails on Weber Street, thanks to Max.

Neatnik Nicky washes windows with vinegar, water, and lots of elbow grease. We can see the scene clearly on Weber Street.

Ava's our computer whiz. She helps Mrs. Cline keep up with all her friends online.

From Weber Street,
Mrs. Cline reaches
the whole world,
thanks to Ava!

Barney can make
the Barkley babies laugh,
even at their grumpiest.

All of us on Weber Street are grateful.

Sam and Len are the Garage Guys.

They help clear up clutter that would spill out onto Weber Street.

On garbage day, the Weber Street
Wonder Work Crew
is on the job.

Mr. Ambrosia is glad to have help from Amy and Rosie taking his recycling to the curb.

Ross and Rob are responsible for gathering up mail and flyers and newspapers while the Hendersons are on vacation.

This helps keep Weber Street safe.

Today's the Weber Street block sale.

We've been putting on prices,

making change,

and packing up purchases all day.

And tonight's the best time of all –
the Weber Street Barbecue!
We all pitch in with the work
and the fun!